Front jacket: The Basset Hound is descended from the Bloodhound and despite its heavy body and short legs is remarkably agile.

Front endpapers: The German Shepherd is one of the most versatile working dogs.

DOGS

Above: Even the larger mastiff breeds are able to lower their fierce guard
occasionally, and pose for pictures like this!

DOGS
Angela Sayer

Contents

Introduction   6-7

Puppies   8-19

Your Family Dog   20-33

The Prizewinners   34-47

Action Dogs   48-64

Left: A team of German Shepherd dogs make little of an obstacle placed across their path, demonstrating their fantastic jumping ability and complete obedience to their trainer.

Previous page: Large sleds can require teams of at least 13 dogs, often more, to haul them quickly over snow and ice.

This book was devised and produced by
Multimedia Publications (UK) Ltd

Editor **Richard Rosenfeld**
Design **Behram Kapadia**
Picture Research **Maggie Colbeck**
Production **Arnon Orbach**

ISBN 0-8317-2399-8

First published in the United States of America 1984 by Gallery Books, an imprint of W. H. Smith Publishers Inc., 112 Madison Avenue, New York, NY 10016

Originated by D S Colour International Ltd, London
Typeset by Rowland Phototypesetting (London) Ltd
Printed in Spain by Cayfosa, Barcelona
Dep. Legal B-30.099 - 1984

Introduction

Though scientists disagree about the exact ancestry and evolution of today's domestic dog, it is generally believed that the process of domestication began at least 12 000 years ago. This theory is supported by a fairly recent discovery in Israel of a fossilized skeleton of a man, his hand resting on the head of his dog, stretched out at his side. It also seems likely there was a very close relationship between early tribes and dogs, with the hunters relying on dog packs to corner prey. The hunters then stepped in and killed the animal, leaving the remains for the dogs.

War dogs

It did not take people long to realize that the dog could be a very useful ally, which could be successfully trained to help carry out specific tasks. Various archaeological finds, cave paintings and temple carvings show dogs working or playing with humans. Tall, wolf-like dogs appear to have accompanied archers of Paleolithic times and huge mastiff-like dogs went to war with the soldiers depicted in Babylonian works of about 2500 BC, while the ancient Egyptian Pharaohs favored tall sleek dogs very similar to today's sight hounds.

Today, there are approximately 200 dog breeds; they come in an amazing range of colors, shapes and sizes, from the mighty mastiffs to the diminutive toy breeds. They are also used for a wide variety of purposes, including hunting, as watch dogs, on the race track, hauling sleds across miles of frozen country, for herding stock and aiding the blind. Dogs are also used by the military to carry supplies and messages across mine-fields, and by the police for catching criminals, controling crowds and detecting drugs and explosives.

Inseparable companions

Dogs and man have become almost inseparable throughout the world. The animal's natural, protective instinct makes it the perfect guard for the family and the home, factory, farm or store, but its most important role is that of pet and companion, when it comes into its own as quiet comforter, silent confidante and special friend.

Left: Originally called the Russian Wolfhound because a Russian aristocrat imported them from Arabia in the early part of the seventeenth century, the Borzoi is a breed of elegant appearance. It also possesses speed, intelligence, courage and a strong will.

Puppies

A puppy is the name given to a young dog from birth until it reaches about one year of age, when it is considered to be adult. Puppies are born after a nine-week gestation period, and are helpless, blind and almost deaf at birth. During the first 12 weeks of life, however, there are many developments: the puppy learns a great deal about life and absorbs information at an amazing rate.

Maternal bond

All puppies develop at slightly different rates, but their general patterns are similar. From birth until the eyes open at 10 to 16 days, the puppy is said to be in the *neonatal* stage. During this time the bitch-puppy bond is at its strongest. The mother feeds and cleans the puppy, licking away all wastes and keeping the nest spotlessly clean.

The puppy sleeps for about nine-tenths of the time, waking only to be fed and cleaned, and its actions are governed by a series of reflexes, all of which are designed to keep it as close as possible to its mother's body for safety, nourishment and warmth.

The eyes open at the onset of the *transitional* stage, but do not blink or focus properly for a while – hearing is also weak at this time. The puppy's leg and body muscles grow steadily stronger so that it is able to stand and move both forward and back. At three weeks the puppy enters the *socialization* stage, and this important period lasts until it is 10 weeks old. During this time the puppy is weaned, and begins to acquire different behavioral patterns.

Leaving home

From three to four weeks, the puppy sleeps less and feeds more. It shows its first playful signs and reacts to various stimuli from its mother, littermates and humans.

Although puppies are able to eat solids from the age of three weeks or so, the bitch continues to feed them until the litter is six to eight weeks old. Once weaning is complete, puppies are ready to go to new homes. From the tenth week, the puppy enters its *juvenile* phase, which lasts until it reaches sexual maturity, when it is considered to have become adult.

Left: Like all puppies, these Basset Hounds are quite irresistible, and when adult will help hunt for hare, fox and pheasant. When choosing a dog it is vital to take into account its adult size, likely temperament and exercise requirements.

Above: A patient bitch of the Basset Griffon Vendéen
variety nurses her strong litter of five puppies. Four
types of Basset Hound were bred in France after the
days of the Revolution. To enable people to hunt on
foot, rather than on horseback, a strong hound with
shorter legs was required and the Basset Hounds
admirably met their needs.

Right: Most working dogs produce and rear their puppies in a straw or hay nest in the corner of a barn or stable. The puppies are kept clean, warm and dry, and grow up hardy and very healthy away from artificial heat. Here, a working sheepdog bitch romps with her two puppies as they learn to play-fight.

Below: The same pups learn to take solid food. Some owners feed each puppy individually, but here this litter shares a communal bowl. The stimulus of competition obviously encourages them to eat everything. Puppies grow rapidly at this stage and need nourishing meals. When adult, the Basset Griffon Vendéen is used for hunting boar and deer.

Left: Hound puppies are particularly sociable and enjoy constant fun and games with other pups, especially when they have room to run and romp in a large outdoor area.

Below: All puppies are appealing, but these little Bassets with their soulful eyes and drooping ears look particularly vulnerable. Generally, it is not a good idea to put young puppies onto chairs or anything they can easily fall from. Breeds with heavy bones may receive permanent injuries from falls suffered at this critical age.

Above: Like all gundog puppies, these month-old golden retrievers are cute and cuddly. However, potential owners must remember that they will grow up to become tall, strong dogs which require a considerable amount of regular exercise in order to stay fit, healthy and in good condition. Gundog breeds ideally need spacious homes in the country.

Above: Usually children and puppies play well together but to prevent accidents, children need careful instruction about the special needs and frailties of young animals.

Right: A terrier breed which makes an ideal house pet is the West Highland White. It is a good choice for families with children who should be taught that the dog must never be teased in case it retaliates with a quick bite. The "westie" repays correct early training and is a good house dog, with a loud deep bark.

Below: Two small breeds – the miniature smoothcoated Dachshund on the left of the picture, and the Yorkshire Terrier on the right. Small breeds like these need careful rearing and handling in their early days, but grow up to be surprisingly tough adults.

Above: The Boxer is a relatively new breed having been developed in Germany in the middle of the nineteenth century from the bulldog and the mastiff. Despite its somewhat fierce appearance, the Boxer is a delightfully docile creature.

Left: Puppies born and raised on a farm, like these little Retrievers, always seem to have far more opportunities for fun and play than those raised elsewhere. The Golden Retriever is a very reliable gundog both on land and in the water, and its patient temperament makes it a particularly good companion for children.

Above: All Poodle puppies resemble powder puffs as soon as their eyes open. The coat forms soft curls and waves from the tips of their ears to the ends of their tails. It is at this age that some breeders start to clip the faces of the dogs.

Right: This handsome litter of Standard Poodle puppies is a little older than the litter of Toy Poodle pups above. They have had their faces neatly clipped, just like their mother's. It is difficult to believe that in the past the Poodle was used in France as a retriever.

Left: Border Collie pups aged 14 weeks. Border Collies are one of the easiest breeds of dog to train.

Below: Boundless energy, stamina, strength and tenacity – all traits which are obviously apparent in these Australian cattle dog puppies, even at this tender age. Several working breeds were combined to produce this superlative cattle dog, including two extinct sheepdog breeds, the Black Bobtail and the Smithfield Drover, as well as the Dingo – the wild Australian dog.

Above: The Beagle is the smallest of the pack hounds and was developed for hunting hares, on foot. Today, Beagles are immensely popular as pets, but many owners forget that they are taking into their homes extremely energetic, lively and extrovert hounds. With lots of exercise and careful training, however, Beagles make fine pets.

Your Family Dog

The pedigree dogs are generally placed in one of two groups: Sporting Breeds and Non-Sporting Breeds. The first group consists of all the hounds, the terriers, and the gundogs, while the second group contains all breeds used for guarding or herding, companion breeds and toy breeds.

Sporting breeds

Most of the dogs in the sporting group need lots of daily exercise to keep fit. The dogs which have silky "feather" on the legs and tail also have long hair on the ears and this needs daily grooming. Few gundogs make good guards, they are far too friendly, and most of them are gentle with children. Terriers are all fairly similar in temperament – quick, agile and alert with fast reactions which can make them appear rather snappy. Wiry-coated terriers need regular hand-stripping or trimming, which must be carried out by an expert. The scent hounds rarely make good pets because they require enormous amounts of exercise and can run for hours at a stretch. The sight hounds like the Afghan and Saluki can be very aloof and have strong hunting instincts. They also need a lot of exercise and regular grooming.

Non-sporting breeds

In the non-sporting group there are various sub-divisions. The working section covers such breeds as the Alsatian or German Shepherd Dog, the Boxer, Collies, Corgies and guard dogs such as the Dobermann Pinscher, plus the big mastiff breeds, Newfoundland, Pyrenean Mountain Dog, St Bernard and Great Dane.

The utility section covers breeds like the Poodle, the Bulldog and the Dalmatian. Tiny breeds like the Chihuahua and the Pekinese belong to the toy group. Toy breeds are inexpensive to keep and take up very little space. Their size detracts from their worth as guards but they make good, "noisy" watchdogs. Few toy breeds are suitable for homes with young children. Most of the herding breeds make very good guard dogs and are ideal with children.

Some cross-bred dogs make excellent family pets. Their potential depends greatly on the breeds in their ancestry and their early temperament as puppies. All dogs repay early care and affection and require methodical training.

Left: Always set apart a number of hours each day to play with and exercise your dog. Without exercise, he will become listless and bad tempered.

Left: A Golden Retriever begs beautifully for his young owner. This breed is one of the very best for families with young children. It is easy to train, not only in basic obedience, but also to perform a few tricks, to fetch and carry and, naturally, to retrieve. Unless used as a working dog, it needs exercise to prevent obesity.

Below: It is extraordinary how different kinds of animals can tolerate each other, even play together, like this otter and dog romping in the snow. If treated properly, many dogs can be trained to live quite happily with a vast assortment of animals.

Above: Collies, both pure and crossbred, have an
inborn guarding instinct and are often very protective
of property and their owners' personal possessions.

Above: These beautiful Borzois or Russian Wolfhounds obviously accompany their owners wherever they go. Dogs left in cars must always have access to fresh air to prevent them becoming too hot.

Borzois used to hunt wolves so they require a great •deal of regular exercise. They are bred in many colors from white to black and tan.

Right: Dogs, like humans, are social animals, so many enjoy the opportunity to meet, mix and play with others of their kind. Here a group of people accompanied by their dogs enjoy a country walk.

Below: Many dogs, particularly those of the working breeds, enjoy swimming and playing in water. It is important to watch your dog when it swims in the sea because it may become disorientated and swim out too far, or return to the beach some way from where it entered the water. Always rinse salt water from the dog's coat as soon as possible.

Above: This lively dog tries to retrieve his ball from the swimming pool. Some dogs, however, are frightened of water and should on no account be forced to jump in if they do not want to.

Above: Dogs can be taught a great variety of tricks. It certainly does not do them any harm – in fact the more time you spend training your dog the livelier and happier he will be.

Left: This boy definitely picked the right breed for a swimming companion. The Poodle was first bred as a gundog to retrieve wildfowl, and was known as the Water Dog or *Pudel* of Germany. Most poodles retain their love of water and are excellent swimmers as well as being highly intelligent, easy to train and very loyal to their owners.

Below: The fitting of a dog door into a safely enclosed garden or yard enables the dog to come and go as it pleases. The door selected should be high and wide enough to prevent any stripping of the dog's coat, and the base of the door must be sited low enough to allow an easy step-over for older dogs.

Above: All dogs love to chew and, like this fawn Whippet, are adept at holding sticks and bones between their paws. Make sure chewing objects will not splinter and cause injury. The Whippet is a descendant of a cross between a terrier, an Italian Greyhound and a Greyhound. It is very fast and can reach speeds exceeding 30 mph.

Above: This perky Fox Terrier enjoys a drink from the water spout after a brisk walk in the hot sun. Dogs require regular cooling drinks during spells of hot weather; their coats need regular stripping by an expert. The Fox Terrier is a very good watchdog and an excellent companion.

Above: Never treat an injured dog yourself – always take it straight to the vet to have it properly cared for. This well bandaged Norfolk terrier is one of the smallest breeds of terrier and has only recently been officially recognized. Its coat varies through all shades of red to black and tan.

Above: The Golden Retriever is a perfect pet. Easily trained it is obedient and very loving but requires lots of exercise to keep fit and regular grooming to keep the coat in condition. The coat can be many shades of cream or gold and has a water-resistant undercoat. Golden Retrievers are fairly large dogs weighing up to 70 pounds.

Right: Not all dogs are loved and cared for. Some become strays and, unless caught and found new homes, may join a feral pack. Here, two dogs in poor condition forage for food scraps among the garbage. Stray dogs should be taken to a local humane society office or dog pound, or, if they cannot be caught, reported to the authorities.

Below: Unlike the unfortunate stray dogs, this Labrador Retriever is obviously the constant and devoted companion of its young master. Here is the dog-man relationship at its best – shared solitude without the need for words, praise or commands. The Labrador is one of the kindest and gentlest of breeds, fearless and intelligent.

The Prizewinners

Dog shows are big business in several countries. Britain has the largest dog shows with entries of about 10 000 animals in each of six or seven major events, while in the United States and Australia large shows often attract around 4000 competing dogs. Every country has separate classes for dogs and bitches and these are divided into classes for puppies, maiden and novice dogs, debutantes, undergraduates, graduates, post-graduates, limit, and open. Eligibility depends on awards previously won.

The winners

Dogs compete in their individual classes, then the winners parade before the judge who selects the Best Dog, then the Best Bitch. Best Dog and Best Bitch compete for the Best of Breed title. Best of Breed winners are then judged within their relevant groups and a Best of Group award is given to each winner – Best Hound, Best Gundog, Best Terrier, Best Utility, Best Working, and Best Toy. From the six group winners will be chosen the Best in Show.

Judging is an acquired art. Each judge must be an expert in the breeds in which he officiates. Each breed of dog has a written standard of points which describes every feature of the dog's conformation: coat structure, color and pattern and its faults which are penalized. The standard for each breed is drawn up by the society concerned.

International standards

In Britain a dog must win three Challenge Certificates from three different judges, one Certificate at least after he has attained one year of age, to gain the champion title. In the United States a dog must accumulate 15 points, and the points available at each show depend on the entry. In Europe dogs must win special Certificates of Aptitude Championship International and Beauty (CACIB). Four such Certificates must be won under three different judges and in at least three different countries. Commonwealth countries with the exception of Canada work on a system very similar to that of Britain, and the Canadian show system requires the award of 10 points under three different judges to make a canine champion.

Left: On the right are two champion Boxers. The German Shepherd on the left is one of the best known guard dogs. It can also be trained to sniff out drugs and explosives, control criminals and help to rescue people.

Above: Some breeds require a great deal of show preparation before entering the ring, for correct presentation can decide the final decision between two or more dogs of equally good conformation.

This Standard Poodle, already clipped and bathed, has the hair of its topknot and ears braided to keep it clean and in shape until its class is called.

Right: The judge makes his final decision, having chosen his best dogs. He must take into account the official standard of points for the breed and employ his expert skills to assess every part of the dog's conformation, including the coat's structure, color and pattern. And, of course, the dog's faults must be penalized.

Below: Cruft's Dog Show, held in London, England, during February, is a major event for the dog fanciers of the world who flock to see dogs of all breeds competing over a three-day period. Here in the ring, Pyrenean Mountain Dogs are paraded by their proud owners before the presiding judge and her steward who mark their judging books.

Left: Most Spaniel breeds enjoy shows and showing. They are typically lively, extrovert dogs and move with natural grace. Spaniels do need considerable show preparation, however. Their coats must be clean with full feathering on the legs and ears well furnished with silky hairs.

Below: An interesting line-up of Terriers at Cruft's Dog Show. Most Terrier breeds originated in Britain and records go back to the fifteenth century. The name came from *terra,* the Latin word for earth, because the little dogs were used mainly for digging out vermin of various kinds which had taken refuge from humans and dogs, beneath the ground.

Right: At the larger shows, dogs are given their own numbered benches on which they are required to sit or rest until called to their classes. This enables visitors to the show to check the dogs' numbers against their show catalogues for identification. These strikingly marked dogs are harlequin Great Danes.

Below: A line-up of Old English Sheepdogs at the Southern Counties Dog Show in England. It is easy to see why these dogs have become such popular pets, but owners must remember to brush their coats regularly.

Left: Some dog shows are held out doors, and in warm weather such shows attract many visitors. Small dogs are generally judged on a raised bench or table, enabling the judge to examine each entrant thoroughly after seeing it move, on the lead, in the ring.

Below: Top awards at Cruft's Dog Show are eagerly sought by top breeders, and after the open breed classes, winners compete for Best of Group awards. Here we see the final judging in the Terrier group in which the magnificent cup has been won by a wonderful West Highland White, while the runner-up is a beautiful white Bull Terrier.

Above: The Saluki makes an excellent show dog. It is an ancient member of the Greyhound family, a coursing dog of the Bedouin, and sometimes referred to as the Gazelle Hound. This beautiful dog can be up to 28 inches tall and weigh up to 66 pounds. The Saluki is also a surprisingly good watchdog.

Left: Popular as a show dog, the Afghan Hound was first used in its native country of Afghanistan as a guard at night, and to hunt wolves and deer during the day. Its very long, silky coat requires special preparation for the show ring, a good diet and regular grooming.

Left: The Shetland Islands off the north coast of Scotland have produced distinctive and hardy small breeds of sheep and pony and the Shetland Sheepdog developed naturally as a working dog similar to the much larger Rough Collie. Little is known of its exact ancestry, but the "Sheltie" of today makes a good pet, when carefully trained, and a fine show dog.

Right: The West Highland White Terrier was first called the Poltalloch, and has always been a pure white breed. It was first developed for hunting foxes in rough and rocky terrain where a bold, brave and agile dog was required; today's "westie" has retained all these characteristics.

Left: The Dogue de Bordeaux may be considered the national dog of France. It is similar to the English Mastiff and is descended from the same root stock as all other mastiff breeds, the Romans' war dogs. This big and placid dog is loyal to its family, making a good guard as well as a show dog.

Below: A family group of yellow Labrador Retrievers pose in the ground of a great English country house. Dogs of this breed have long been favored by countrymen because they are excellent working gundogs and kind pets. Labradors are very intelligent and easy to train.

Above: The Gazelle Hound has remained unchanged in color and shape for thousands of years. It is renowned for its grace and speed.

Above: The Shar-Pei, or Chinese Fighting Dog, is recorded as being the world's rarest breed of dog, and one of its characteristics is a skin that looks several sizes too large. It can be black, red, cream, or fawn in color and is thought to be a descendant of the Chow-Chow.

Right: Another strange and rare eastern breed is the Chinese Crested. It is a dainty, intelligent little dog quite hairless on the body, but with hair on the paws and tail, and over the head and neck, forming a distinctive crest. The skin needs care and should be rubbed with baby oil to prevent coarseness and cracking. Sunburn must be avoided.

Below: A fairly rare breed, popular in the show ring, is the Puli or Hungarian Water Dog. Usually black or brindled, the Puli has an unusual coat which hangs to the ground in thick cords. The Puli is one of the smaller sheepdogs. It is a highly intelligent and easily trained breed, a good watchdog and an unusual pet.

Action Dogs

The dog has proved a willing worker since its domestication.

Perhaps the oldest of the dog's functions, apart from natural hunting, is herding. Many of the breeds that were first developed as herding dogs showed a natural guarding potential. Certain breeds, however, such as the German Shepherd, have been found to have other attributes making them suitable for a wide range of duties. Some herding dogs such as the Border Collie, work by eye contact. Others, such as the Hungarian Puli, work vocally, while some, such as the bustling Welsh Corgi, work by nipping at the heels of the stock which they are moving.

Special abilities

Many breeds excel as watchdogs, and some have been developed with special abilities so that they are ideal for use in rescue work, police work and as dogs of war. Such breeds include the Dobermann Pinscher, the Rottweiler, the Weimaraner, and the Schnauzer. The German Shepherd, of course, excels in this field, and it also makes a good guide dog for the blind. Labrador and Golden Retrievers make superb guide dogs, and are also used as hearing dogs for the deaf. Bitches are generally selected as guide dogs. They are less easily distracted than male dogs, despite the fact that guide dogs are neutered before starting their training.

Hunters

Various types of hound are used for hunting. There are Foxhounds, Staghounds, Harriers and Draghounds, all of which are followed on horseback. Beagles and Bassets are followed on foot. Staghounds hunt red deer, Foxhounds hunt the red fox and Harriers, Beagles and Bassets hunt jack rabbits and other small game. Bloodhounds are followed on horseback or on foot and pursue a trail laid by a runner. Working trials for these hounds are held under the rules of both the American and the British Kennels Clubs.

The gundog groups all work in their own distinctive ways, some finding game, some merely retrieving game gunned down by their masters, some both find and retrieve. Terriers are used for hunting animals such as rats and rabbits which are considered farm pests.

Left: The Pointer is a large dog, thought to have been first bred in Spain. It is obedient, easily trained and makes an excellent gundog on grasslands and moor.

Left: At a rough shoot, the dogs are a vital part in the day's sport, bringing in the game as they fall to the guns. Pictured is a remarkable retrieve as the dog accurately gauges and clears a wire strand, above a high mesh fence, after retrieving the bird. A soft mouth is essential to avoid damaging the game.

Right: Spaniels have a longer history than any other gundog group, and were first used in Spain to drive game birds through the undergrowth and into waiting nets. They are versatile and easily trained dogs. The Springer Spaniel, shown here, makes a superb retriever on land. It is also an excellent water dog, tireless and eager.

Below: A German Shorthaired Pointer marking game in the stubble field. This breed was developed from the early Spanish pointers and indigenous bird dogs as a dual-purpose animal to point and retrieve game. Dogs of this breed may be either a "solid" liver color, or any combination of liver with white, spotted or ticked. The coat is short and hard.

Left: The Kelpie, or Australian Sheepdog, is perhaps the world's most energetic working dog. It lives mainly on farms in its native land, rounding up sheep and separating them on command for the administration of medicines, vaccinations, docking and shearing. The Kelpie was bred from various Scottish Sheepdogs and to the busy sheep farmer the dog is worth his weight in gold.

Below: Seen here working a full flock of sheep is a Briard, a breed used extensively for this work in France. It is a long-coated dog which may be of any color but is most often seen in black or slate gray. Its name comes from the province of Brie where it was developed as a guard/herder in the nineteenth century.

Above: A delightful pastoral scene as the shepherd, aided by his two Collies, moves his flock in the early hours of the morning. Collies were first named after black-faced Scottish colley sheep. Collies make excellent watchdogs and are particularly protective toward their owners.

Left: A sled dog and her pup wait for their food, seemingly impervious to the snow and cold. Although all sled dogs are commonly referred to as "huskies," only one of the four recognized varieties of northern draught dogs should have this title and that is the Siberian Husky – an impressive dog with a double coat and great powers of endurance.

Below: Pictured in an Eskimo village in Greenland. Two sled dogs chew meat from the jawbone of a recently butchered whale. The Eskimo dog, called the Kingmik, originated in Greenland and for many years provided the only form of transportation in that remote land. Such dogs make effective guards.

Above: Even with modern forms of transportation readily available; the dog-team tour is offered as a popular optional extra. The Siberian Husky was brought to Alaska at the beginning of the twentieth century. In the United States and Canada, the Husky now takes part in the popular pastime of sled-racing.

Left: This German Shepherd Dog is being trained to attack on command, and is set to chase, attack and hold the "enemy". The trainer's assistant has his right arm protected by a steel and leather guard covered with soft padding because the dog is trained to hold the right arm.

Below: In the military, dogs are trained to perform a very wide variety of tasks. As well as carrying messages and supplies across enemy lines, they are used to guard property and personnel. Here a dog is being baited by the trainer's assistant to make him as protective as possible.

Right: This police handler is putting his fully trained German Shepherd Dog through its paces during a special display. Police dogs perform their routines before audiences at dog shows, community shows and country fairs, often to raise money for charities.

Below: The dog handler's assistant pretends here to be a criminal. When cornered, he baits and taunts the dog, making it increasingly angry. When a real-life criminal is faced with such ferocity it shouldn't be too long before he gives himself up.

Above: At an annual public show, one of Britain's
Royal Air Force dogs shows that there is a lighter side
to the stringent training routines it must undergo.

58

Above: This dog is being fitted with a special harness, enabling him to be hoisted up or lowered by the helicopter winch. The helicopter is fitted with equipment to enable it to land on snow, and the whole operation is designed to search for and rescue climbers, mountaineers and travelers who are lost in blizzards or avalanches.

Right: On arrival at the scene of an accident or avalanche, a trained rescue dog and his handler are carefully lowered by winch from the helicopter. The dog must be trained so that it does not struggle or upset its balance during the descent. It is skilled in finding lost humans buried under a deep layer of snow.

Left: A pack of Foxhounds sets off through the early morning mist. Foxhounds were first employed to hunt foxes towards the end of the seventeenth century in Sussex, England. The hounds were bred from the Northern Hound, a type of Deerhound, and the Southern Hound, descended from the European Talbots. Later, some Greyhound blood was added to give the hounds extra speed.

Right: This exciting picture shows a contestant in the Iditarod sled race, an annual event in which teams of dogs race in three to four days from Nome, Alaska over a distance of 400 miles.

Below: Greyhounds race round the track in pursuit of a mechanical hare. The Greyhound possesses great stamina, is built for speed and is probably the fastest dog over short distances.

Above: During an impressive display of dog-training techniques a team of handlers here seen with their German Shepherd dogs, demonstrate group discipline and obedience to simple voice commands and hand signals. The same gestures and commands should always be used when training a dog and orders should be delivered in a calm, patient voice.

Right: The massive alpine mastiff, known as the St Bernard, found fame as a rescue dog in the Swiss Alps at the end of the eighteenth century. Today the breed is popular as a show dog. It is strong and self-willed, needing lots of space, plenty of food and adequate exercise.

Below: A German Shepherd dog jumps through a blazing hoop, so demonstrating its fearlessness. First developed for herding purposes from the sheepdogs of Bavaria, the German Shepherd, also known as the Alsatian, made its first show appearance in 1826. After this it rapidly gained in popularity and proved its worth as a watchdog, guide and working dog.

Above: A fine head study of a magnificent St Bernard pictured in a typical alpine setting. It bears the traditional barrel of cognac around its neck to revive lost travelers. St Bernards are very large dogs, weighing between 110 and 120 pounds and standing at least 25 inches in height. They are still used in mountain rescue work.

Picture Credits

Back jacket: The Collie is best known as an excellent sheepdog.

Back endpapers: Fox Terriers are very energetic dogs and need a well balanced diet.